Behold A Savior is Born

A Scriptural Account of the Birth of Jesus Christ

Compilation by:
Natalie Ellis & Jonathan Ellis

© 2026 Natalie Ellis & Jonathan Ellis
Grove Media
All rights reserved.
No part of this book may be reproduced, stored in a retrieval system, or transmitted in any form or by any means—electronic, mechanical, photocopying, recording, or otherwise—except for brief quotations for reviews or educational purposes, without prior written permission from the publisher.

Scriptural passages in this book are quoted from the Holy Bible and the Book of Mormon.
Biblical passages are from The King James translations.
Book of Mormon passages are quoted from the standard text of The Book of Mormon: Another Testament of Jesus Christ.
The selection, arrangement, and presentation of these scriptures, as well as all illustrations and design elements, are original to this work.

This book is intended for devotional, educational, and family reading purposes.
No commentary, paraphrasing, or interpretation has been added to the scriptural text.

First Edition
Printed in the United States of America
ISBN: 978-1-969494-06-2

Behold A SAVIOR IS BORN

Prophesy of the Messiah's Birth

740-700 BC - Israel, in or near Jerusalem

Isaiah 7:14
Therefore the Lord himself shall give you a sign; Behold a virgin shall conceive, and bear a son, and shall call his name Immanuel.

Isaiah 9:6
For unto us a child is born, unto us a son is given: and the government shall be upon his shoulder: and his name shall be called Wonderful, Counsellor, The mighty God, The everlasting Father, The Prince of Peace.

Micah 5:2
But thou, Bethlehem Ephratah, though thou be little among the thousands of Judah, yet out of thee shall He come forth unto me that is to be ruler in Israel; whose goings forth have been from of old, from everlasting.

---

82 BC - Americas, in or near Zarahemla

Alma 7:9
... for behold the kingdom of heaven is at hand, and the Son of God cometh upon the face of the earth.

Alma 7:10
And behold, he shall be born of Mary, at Jerusalem which is the land of our forefathers, she being a virgin, a precious and chosen vessel, who shall be overshadowed and conceive by the power of the Holy Ghost, and bring forth a son, yea, even the Son of God.

Prophesy of the Messiah's Birth

6 BC - Americas, city wall of Zarahemla

Helaman 14:1
And now it came to pass that Samuel, the Lamanite, did prophesy a great many more things which cannot be written.

Helaman 14:2
And behold, he said unto them: Behold, I give unto you a sign; for five years more cometh, and behold, then cometh the Son of God to redeem all those who shall believe on his name.

Helaman 14:3
And behold, this will I give unto you for a sign at the time of his coming; for behold, there shall be great lights in heaven, insomuch that in the night before he cometh there shall be no darkness, insomuch that it shall appear unto man as if it was day.

Helaman 14:4
Therefore, there shall be one day and a night and a day, as if it were one day and there were no night; and this shall be unto you for a sign; for ye shall know of the rising of the sun and also of its setting; therefore they shall know of a surety that there shall be two days and a night; nevertheless the night shall not be darkened; and it shall be the night before he is born.

PROPHESY OF THE MESSIAH'S BIRTH

6 BC - Americas, city wall of Zarahemla

Helaman 14:5
And behold, there shall a new star arise, such an one as ye never have beheld; and this also shall be a sign unto you.

Helaman 14:6
And behold this is not all, there shall be many signs and wonders in heaven.

Helaman 14:8
And it shall come to pass that whosoever shall believe on the Son of God, the same shall have everlasting life.

The Annunciation

Luke 1:26
And in the sixth month the angel Gabriel was sent from God unto a city of Galilee, named Nazereth,

Luke 1:27
To a virgin espoused to a man whose name was Joseph, of the house of David; and the virgin's name was Mary.

Luke 1:28
And the angel came in unto her, and said, Hail, thou that art highly favoured, the Lord is with thee: blessed art thou among women.

Luke 1:29
And when she saw him, she was troubled at his saying, and cast in her mind what manner of salutation this should be.

Luke 1:30
And the angel said unto her, Fear not, Mary: for thou hast found favour with God.

Luke 1:31
And, behold, thou shalt conceive in the womb, and bring forth a son, and shalt call his name JESUS.

Luke 1:32
He shall be great, and shall be called the Son of the Highest: and the Lord God shall give unto him the throne of his father David:

The Annunciation

Luke 1:34
Then said Mary unto the angel, How shall this be, seeing I know not a man?

Luke 1:35
And the angel answered and said unto her, The Holy Ghost shall come upon thee, and the power of the Highest shall overshadow thee: therefore also that holy thing which shall be born of thee shall be called the Son of God.

Luke 1:37
For with God nothing shall be impossible.

Luke 1:38
And Mary said, Behold the handmaid of the Lord; be it unto me according to they word. And the angel departed from her.

The Annunciation

Matthew 1:18
Now the birth of Jesus Christ was on this wise: When as his mother Mary was espoused to Joseph, before they came together, she was found with child of the Holy Ghost.

Matthew 1:20
But while he thought on these things, behold, the angel of the Lord appeared unto him in a dream, saying, Joseph, thou son of David, fear not to take unto thee Mary thy wife: for that which is conceived in her is of the Holy Ghost.

Matthew 1:21
And she shall bring forth a son, and thou shalt call his name JESUS: for he shall save his people from their sins.

Matthew 1:24
Then Joseph being raised from sleep did as the angel of the Lord had bidden him, and took unto him his wife:

Matthew 1:25
And knew her not till she had brought forth her firstborn son: and he called his name JESUS.

Journey to Bethlehem

Luke 2:1
And it came to pass in those days, that there went out a decree from Caesar Augustus, that all the world should be taxed.

Luke 2:3
And all went to be taxed, every one into his own city.

Luke 2:4
And Joseph also went up from Galilee, out of the city of Nazareth, into Judaea, unto the city of David, which is called Bethlehem; (because he was of the house and lineage of David:)

Luke 2:5
To be taxed with mary his espoused wife, being great with child.

THE BIRTH OF JESUS CHRIST

Americas

3 Nephi 1:9
Now it came to pass that there was a day set apart by the unbelievers, that all those who believed in those traditions should be put to death except the sign should come to pass, which had been given by Samuel the prophet.

the voice of the Lord came unto him, saying:
3 Nephi 1:13
Lift up your head and be of good cheer; for behold, the time is at hand, and on this night shall the sign be given, and on the morrow come I into the world, to show unto the world that I will fulfil all that which I have caused to be spoken by the mouth of my holy prophets.

Bethlehem

Luke 2:6
And so it was, that, while they were there, the days were accomplished that she should be delivered.

Luke 2:7
And she brought forth her firstborn son, and wrapped him in swaddling clothes, and laid him in a manger; because there was no room for them in the inn.

The Shepherds

Luke 2:8
And there were in the same country shepherds abiding in the field, keeping watch over their flock by night.

Luke 2:9
And, lo, the angel of the Lord came upon them, and the glory of the Lord shone round about them: and they were sore afraid.

Luke 2:10
And the angel said unto them, Fear not: for, behold, I bring you good tidings of great joy, which shall be to all people.

Luke 2:11
For unto you is born this day in the city of David a Saviour, which is Christ the Lord.

Luke 2:12
And this shall be a sign unto you: Ye shall find the babe wrapped in swaddling clothes, lying in a manger.

Luke 2:13
And suddenly there was with the angel a multitude of the heavenly host praising God, and saying,

Luke 2:14
Glory to God in the highest, and on earth peace, good will toward men.

THE SHEPHERDS

Luke 2:15
And it came to pass, as the angels were gone away from them into heaven, the shepherds said one to another, let us now go even unto Bethlehem, and see this thing which is come to pass, which the Lord hath made known unto us.

Luke 2:16
And they came with haste, and found Mary, and Joseph, and the babe lying in a manger.

Luke 2:17
And when they had seen it, they made known abroad the saying which was told them concerning this child.

Luke 2:18
And all they that heard it wondered at those things which were told them by the shepherds.

Luke 2:19
But Mary kept all these things, and pondered them in her heart.

Luke 2:20
And the shepherds returned, glorifying and praising God for all the things that they had heard and seen, as it was told unto them.

The Light Goes Forth

Matthew 2:1
Now when Jesus was born in Bethlehem of Judaea in the days of Herod the king, behold, there came wise men from the east to Jerusalem,

Matthew 2:2
Saying, Where is he that is born King of the Jews? for we have seen his star in the east, and are come to worship him.

Matthew 2:9
When they had heard the king, they departed: and, lo, the star, which they saw in the east, went before them, till it came and stood over where the young child was.

Matthew 2:10
When they saw the star, they rejoiced with exceeding great joy.

Matthew 2:11
And when they were come into the house, they saw the young child with Mary his mother, and fell down, and worshipped him: and when they had opened their treasures, they presented unto him gifts; gold, and frankincense, and myrrh.

The Meaning & Why He Came

John 1:14
And the Word was made flesh, and dwelt among us, (and we beheld his glory, the glory as of the only begotten of the Father,) full of grace and truth.

John 3:16
For God so loved the world, that he gave his only begotten Son, that whosoever believeth in him should not perish, but have everlasting life.

Luke 2:30
For mine eyes have seen thy salvation,

Luke 2:31
Which thou hast prepared before the face of all people;

Luke 2:32
A light to lighten the Gentiles, and the glory of thy people Israel.

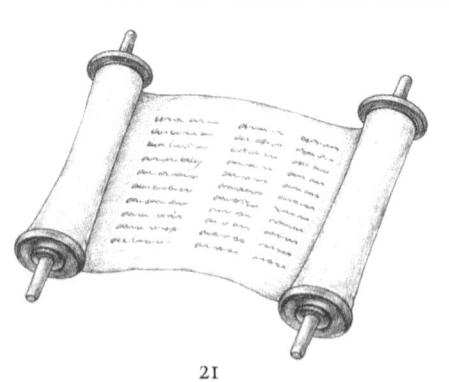

The Meaning & Why He Came

Mosiah 3:5
For behold, the time cometh, and is not far distant, that with power, the Lord Omnipotent who reigneth, who was, and is from all eternity to all eternity, shall come down from heaven among the children of men, and shall dwell in a tabernacle of clay, and shall go forth amongst men, working mighty miracles, such as healing the sick, raising the dead, causing the lame to walk, the blind to receive their sight, and the deaf to hear, and curing all manner of diseases.

Mosiah 3:6
And he shall cast out devils, or the evil spirits which dwell in the hearts of the children of men.

Mosiah 3:7
And lo, he shall suffer temptations, and pain of body, hunger, thirst, and fatigue, even more than man can suffer, except it be unto death; for behold, blood cometh from every pore, so great shall be his anguish for the wickedness and the abominations of his people.

Mosiah 3:8
And he shall be called Jesus Christ, the Son of God, the Father of heaven and earth, the Creator of all things from the beginning; and his mother shall be called Mary.

Our Closing Witness

John 20:31
But these are written, that ye might believe that Jesus is the Christ, the Son of God; and that believing ye might have life through his name.

2 Nephi 25:26
And we talk of Christ, we rejoice in Christ, we preach of Christ, we prophesy of Christ, and we write according to our prophecies, that our children may know to what source they may look for a remission of their sins.

Moroni 10:7
And ye may know that he is, by the power of the Holy Ghost; wherefore I would exhort you that ye deny not the power of God; for he worketh by power, according to the faith of the children of men, the same today and tomorrow, and forever.

About the Authors

For generations, our family has gathered each Christmas Eve to read the story of the Savior's birth from scripture. This tradition began when Natalie was young, passed down from her mother, and has continued as our family has grown. Sitting together, we would take turns reading aloud—most often from the book of Luke.

Over time, we came to realize that while Luke tells much of the story, the witness of the Savior's birth is spread across many books of scripture. This year, as we gathered to read, we found ourselves turning back and forth between passages from the Old Testament, the New Testament, and the Book of Mormon, trying to follow the story in order. In that moment, the thought arose: What if all of these sacred verses were gathered together in one place?

This book was created to do just that—Our hope is that it can be read not only on Christmas Eve, but throughout the days leading up to Christmas, inviting families to gather, read, and center their hearts on Jesus Christ.

Natalie and Jonathan have been married for over twenty-five years and are the parents of two children. Both are creators who find joy in serving and uplifting others. Natalie is an interior and architectural designer and the creator of a motivational podcast focused on wellbeing and healing, inspired by her journey through chronic illness. Jonathan is a middle school teacher, coach, and author of more than twenty children's books, with a passion for motivating and encouraging youth.

This book marks our first collaborative work—and one rooted in the shared belief that Christ is the center of our lives. It is our prayer that this simple gathering of scripture will help families pause, reflect, and rejoice in the true meaning of Christmas.

Enjoy our Easter companion book Behold He is Risen.